2014

The Light You Find

The Light You Find

Terry Martin

Such a pleasure to meet
you at the Northwinds reading.
Here's to acknowledging the shadow,
and celebrating the light.

Terry Martin

Blue Begonia Press   Selah, Washington

ISBN: 978-0-911287-71-4
Cover art: © Bob Fisher, *Rabbit Brush,* 2005.
Cover design by Rob Prout.

Blue Begonia Press
311 Hillcrest Drive Selah, WA
bluebegoniapress.com

Gabriel García Márquez said, "In the end all books are written for your friends." This one is for mine.

Contents

I.

II.

III.

*...carrying through darkness wherever you go
your one little fire that will start again.*

—William Stafford

I

The moment of change is the only poem.

—Adrienne Rich

Backyard

Tonight, out this dark view
from my window, moths
beat dusty wings against
the yellow porch light, and
I'm ten again,
familiar shapes of childhood
appearing through the glass.
Mom's clothesline punctuated
with wooden pins, Dad's
charcoal grill on a scuffed table.
My blue Schwinn Hollywood
leans against Ponderosa Pine,
sister's hula hoop circles a sprinkler.
A green rubber hose coils
like a serpent on wet grass.
In the rock garden, closed buds
of flowers, still clenched.
Lilacs holding promise.
The locked tool shed
waits for the right combination.
Above that back porch, moths
flutter and fling into the fact of lamp.
Up against it, they cannot understand
the heat they are drawn to,
or the light—all they want
just in front of them.

Bedtime

8:00. Still light out. I hear them
playing, their shouting and laughter.
Not me though, sent to bed on schedule,
(and not even tired!) sighing and twisting
in cotton sheets Mom dried on the line.
Lawn mower blades churn—Mr. Harrison, next door?
There's Kelly McGrotha two houses down,
tossing a baseball with his big brother.
Is that Ann Swanson bouncing her
red rubber kickball against their garage?
Miss Lillian Matson yells for her Pekingese,
Yen-Tu, to come in for the night.
And me, alone and apart, stuck inside
this solid safe trap of a house.

Dentist's Waiting Room

You've spotted all the hidden objects—
steam iron nested in tree branches,
scissors merged into fence post,
toaster tucked into hedge.
You've memorized the corny riddles
to tell your little sister later:
Q: Why isn't the ocean musical?
A: Because you can't tune-a-fish.

Envying Goofus, but born to be Gallant,
you wait for your name to be called,
wait for what lies behind that door:
FM music meant to calm,
crinkly paper bib,
sign on the ceiling that says RELAX.
Then, strangest of all,
the lollipop on the way out.

18th & Division

Tall pines guard the house, solid and square.
Oak door speaks directly from the center.
Windows framed in black shutters
stare straight ahead, unflinching.
Brick chimney listens to each word,
and tone of voice matters.

Symmetrical junipers flank the porch,
flat-tops trimmed back with steady hand.
Mowed and edged, the green lawn whispers
Responsibility.

The kind of house my father dreamed of having.
A place where things make sense.
No fists crashing down,
no razor strap bruising
young flesh to toughness.
Where a boy need not stand
between parents, wield a butcher knife,
tell his drunk father
If you hit her again, I'll kill you.

No, if a child left this house
for three days and nights,
someone would surely notice
he'd been gone.

You Are From Here

You are from the boy preacher in a Pentecostal pulpit
and his father's angry fists, from their Alabama
summers and cornbread crumbled in buttermilk.
Unbaptized baby, faith unorganized but deep,
you are from the wooden swing that knocked the girl in the head,
her single seizure, the daily white capsule, red stripe around
its center. From charcoal and acrylics, folded cloth napkins,
grocery lists in perfect penmanship.
You're from Cocoa Puffs, Lysol and Tupperware,
from the steam iron, hissing and spitting.
You're from marbles, jacks, and mumblety peg,
Chinese Checkers and Old Maid. From Beany & Cecil
lunch box, mom's love note tucked inside.
Ducks quacking on Manito Pond, Flexible Flyers
racing down Suicide Hill. From lilac bushes
and Ponderosa Pines, the rock garden
where tulips never grew until your mother's last spring.
You're from reading and impatience,
from Polly and Harvey and Great-Aunt Olive,
from Big Daddy and Nell and drunk Uncle Petty,
run over in front of the Past Time Tavern.
From push lawn mower and pipe tobacco,
tuna casserole and navy bean soup,
library nights and Sunday drives.
Butterick Patterns. Jergens Lotion.
You're from *A Summer Place, Love Me Tender,*
Theme from Exodus, Walk the Line.
From wooden clothespins, cotton sheets flapping.
You are from from Responsibility with a capital R,
from "Give it your best shot and then to hell with it."

Sunday Drive

It starts out like usual, just the four of us,
parents close together in the front seat,
my sister and I silently fighting
over the line we've drawn
between us in back. Me behind Dad,
the nape of his neck clean-cut
and smooth, smelling of Old Spice

when rounding a bend on Old Cheney Road,
we see a beat-up car parked
crooked on the shoulder,
a man and woman standing next to it.
He's hitting her, yelling, slugging her
hard in the face and she's crying.

Dad pulls over, tells us to stay in the car.
My sister and I turn around, kneel against
the backseat to watch through the glass.

When he sees my father,
the man pulls her toward him
screams, red-faced
Why don't you mind your own business?
My father turns to the woman,
tries to get her to come with us.
Please. No. I'm all right. Just go.
"Then I'll stop and call for help."
No. Don't do that, she begs.
Don't do anything.
Just go.

He hesitates for a moment,
then turns around and
walks back to our car.
I stare through the glass at the woman,
her lip split and bleeding,
hollows haunting her face.

The shadow of the man's fist
remains on her cheek.

As we drive away, I watch
the swollen red O of her mouth grow
smaller and smaller in the back window.

Twelve

We went to Sacajawea Junior High.
The cafeteria was a chapel dedicated to striving.
It smelled of corn dogs, tater tots, and fear.
Classrooms were airplanes. We checked for emergency exits.
Buckled our seatbelts, knowing contents might shift.
We took foreign language first period to translate longing.
There was a map of Mexico above Señor Reed's desk.
Risers tiered in the chorus room, permanent
and assured. How we could sing there!
Math was trains. Departures & arrivals. Distance & time.
The librarian, glasses hanging on her bosom from a chain,
was a turkey vulture, casting unexpected shadow.
When the gymnasium doors slammed like fists,
we learned we could survive what hurts.
Girls were excused from showers if they told
Miss Pittock they were having their period.
She marked it on her clipboard chart with a red X.
Like sheep, we gathered, bleating, in Health
with Mr. Frucci, flat-top haircut, corners sharp.
He showed filmstrips on dangers
of tobacco, alcohol and marijuana
on projectors wheeled in and out by audio-visual aides,
earnest, nail-bitten boys, without the distance of irony.
The reading teacher's name was Milo Ball.
We worked on speed and comprehension.
Rumor had it the art teacher was gay.
Shirt buttoned clear up to the top, he stood too close,
rested his hand on the boys' bony shoulders.
In Home Ec we cooked cheese rarebit.
Sewed placemats and gingham aprons.
In woodshop—saws screaming and spitting
golden dust we'd shake from our hair later—
we sanded, hinged, varnished and glued
cedar boxes that smelled like our mothers.
When the bell rang, we spilled
out and converged. Teachers stood in

hallway intersections, reminding us to follow
assigned traffic patterns, keep hands and feet
to ourselves, and pass. Between classes
girls clustered at bathroom mirrors, applying
lipstick, eye shadow and mascara
they would wipe off before going home.
Talked of having zits or not, being invited
or not, French kissing or not.
The principal addressed us in the auditorium
during the convocation on school spirit.
Cheerleaders were 8th graders with breasts.
Notes slipped into lockers held elation and despair.
We didn't know which two or three kids
would be our friends forty years later.
"Meet me behind the water tower"
meant to fight or make out. Mr. B.,
our student teacher in Language Arts/
Social Studies, was young and dreamy.
When it was time for him to leave us,
we pitched in and bought him a paisley necktie.
Our club was The Hesitators.
Our mascot, the chameleon.
Something was going to happen
that would change us.

Fourth Row, Center

The Garland, The Fox, The Majestic.
Lobbies like velvet royalty.
Frescoes and chandeliers.
Carpet so thick I leave footprints.

Behind gleaming counters, popcorn
dances its overpriced jig.
Raisinets, Jujubes, Junior Mints
tiered in bleacher-like rows, root
for The Good Guys, cheering them on.
Licorice whips win out, since
I can make them last longer.

An usher with flashlight leads into the dark.
I follow blindly, trusting his narrow path of light
until, eyes adjusted, I begin to make out
my fellow travelers. Toward front is best.
Trying not to step on toes, I scoot across,
brush knees, stake out my plush seat,
burrow in deep maroon.

My favorite part, then—when heavy drapes open.
As the curtain lifts, my heart does, too.
Music swells feelings that can't be spoken.
Transported by that screen, so much larger
than my one small life.
News for which I've long been homesick.
Stories from someone else's sorrow.

Time stops in that dark,
surrounded by others, side by side,
gazing in the same direction
from separate skins.

That Summer I Read *Dandelion Wine*

A skunk crawled under our shed.
My sister got braces.
I drank Orange Crush.
The radio played "Ol' Black Water"
over and over and over.
Mississippi moon won't you
keep on shinin' on me?
Swans showed up on Manito Pond,
but I preferred the ducks.
Started going to church youth group.
Mostly a chance to be with boys.
On hormonal evenings of flashlight tag,
we circled one another like fireflies.
Played Truth or Dare and Pass the Fizzy.
I wondered if my parents would get to heaven.
And I ain't got no worries
'cause I ain't in no hurry.
That summer Annie Swanson's mom
left her family to be with a woman.
When my dad told me, he said it was sad.
Sad for Annie and her father, her brother and sister?
Or sad that Mrs. Swanson was with a woman?
I poked a hornet's nest under the eaves
with a yellow broom handle.

When My Sister Cut French Class

She dreamed herself wearing a red beret
sipping cappuccino in a Paris café,
speaking the most beautiful language
in the world with ease and grace—
How are you? That's a nice hat.
What time is it? I'd like some cheese, please—
but when my sister cut French class
three days in a row and Monsieur Skinner
gave a surprise test on Friday asking them
to write an essay using the new vocabulary
they had learned that week, all she could
remember was one phrase from Monday—
à toute vitesse—so she began: *I woke up at top speed,*
ate my breakfast at top speed, took the school bus,
which traveled at top speed and so on,
and when she got her test back
a large "F" circled at the top of the page
scrawled in ink red as a beret
was Monsieur's one-line comment:
You must have been exhausted!

The Power of Movies to Disturb

Black-and-white replay: that swarm of screaming birds
pecking Tippi Hedren's eyes, to Tony Perkins' old lady,
smiling, rocking alone in an upstairs room,
to the instrumental theme song of *The Good, The Bad,*
and The Ugly, the cowboy ripping the woman's skirt,
climbing on her, pushing and plunging and grunting
while she cries, your parents thinking you are asleep
in the backseat of the '57 Chevy at the drive-in,
your third-grade brain reeling at this news—a man
can violently take a woman and there is nothing she can do
and nothing you can do—Clint Eastwood does his best
to set things right, but they will never be right.
From the putty-faced bug-eyed psychopath dancin'
in the rain while beating men to bloody pulp
with his cane to Hannibal Lecter with his iceman eyes,
eating a man's liver with some fava beans and a nice Chianti,
hissing *Clarisse,* another snake from the oldest garden
who slithered in and, like the others, took up residence,
tattooed in your mind and forever fearful heart.

What If, Picking Out Her Headstone

your father decides against *Together Forever*
because he might meet someone else someday
and one year later, you're standing up for him
at an outdoor wedding on a coastal island
bearing the ring, oldest daughter giving dad away
in a white gazebo overlooking the sound.
Imagine you and your sister arrived promptly,
to find the new bride had told you to come hours
earlier than necessary, knowing her five kids
always showed up late, assuming his would, too.
Say at the reception, the minister's daughter
jumps at your offer of fifty bucks to write
your toast to the new couple—nothing too flowery
or "One Big Happy Family"—which you
read aloud from a crumpled aqua napkin.
Suppose their smiles seem genuine, hearts joyous.
Picture yourself, impressed and troubled
by how quickly the rest have moved on.

Sorrow

Crows at dawn, so you remember, first thing.
Cracks like thunder, storms your sky.
Rattles and snaps venetian blinds.
Hums in the darkened kitchen.
Screeches and howls at 1 a.m.
Stutters, stammers, searching for words.
Like a rubber band on your wrist,
it snaps your heart, leaving
a raised red welt reminder.

Entering the Question This Night Asks

Again, the dream where teeth loosen
and fall out, one at a time, your raw tongue
prodding the sore, salty spaces they have left.

Resign yourself: you have to do this now.
You may want contact, the certainty of touch,
but understand, it's an inside job.

You won't find it in the next glass of wine,
or the next. Parts may be solved by walking.
And what happens in the hammock helps.

Clues will be given along the way—
weeping limestone, streaked dark,
the razor edge of anger,

words crossing the darkness
to find you, urging you
toward reckoning.

Her Hair Is Red

Beyond taming, ropey tresses ignite—
twisting wildfire, blazing orange.
Green eyes pierce the rippling heat,
pursed red lips smoldering
embers of words held back.
What is she thinking,
this hot-headed woman?
Remembering when sparks first flew?
Recalling an old flame, or
her own burning desire?
Memory erupts into molten lava.
Flames lick the air. Listen.
You can hear her fire crackle.
You can smell the smoke.

Root Canal

The even heaviness of the lead apron
presses down, down.
Then he enters, minty breath and aftershave,
tips my chair back again, shines a bright light,
props my mouth wide open,
shoots in novocaine,
begins poking and prodding and pulling
and I'm as surprised as he is
when tears begin pouring down my cheeks
but, mouth propped, can't tell him why.
Am I hurting you? he asks, alarmed.
I shake my head 'no,' signal him to continue.
I can't tell him that the body remembers
what the mind longs to forget
and for a moment I'm you.
Surgeries, chemo, radiation,
and finally hospice, and the buttery light
of your living room where, in those final days,
you depended on me to do for you
those things you used to do for me.
The stuttering drill mocks me.
Should I stop? he asks again.
Embarrassed, I shake my head.
Keep going, I want to say.
We've all got to just keep going.
Instead, I rub the pastel hem
of my paper bib like a prayer.

Pants on Fire

The lie is a fun-house mirror
that distorts and deceives,
elongating your image like taffy pulled slack,
widening your torso to waddling,
shrinking your head smaller and smaller
until it disappears in the silver.

The lie is a haunted house
with false turns, dead ends.
When skeletons pop out,
and shrieks pierce the dark,
your own bones rattle.

No, the lie is a shadowy forest,
thick with folded fiddlehead ferns.
Clues must have been left along the way,
but you can't find them.
So you doubt yourself.

The lie is a board game without directions,
a puzzle missing pieces, a deck of cards
with no hearts.
It's hard to play for real
without them.

Broom

I like to imagine us far in the future,
when the broom of forgiveness
has swept our past clean.

Dreams

The daughter's heart soars,
a bold and colorful kite,
anchored in the safety
of her mother's closed palm.

Teeth clacking like dominos
fall out one at a time.

You forgot to keep going
to that required statistics class,
so your degree isn't valid.

You're wearing that soft
V-neck lemon-yellow sweater—
the favorite one
you never really had.
In it, you feel strong and lovely.

Mean clowns in a loud circus,
so shiny it hurts your eyes!
The music keeps playing and playing.

Your dead mother returns.
It's up to you to tell her
Dad remarried twenty years ago,
has a new family now.

Flashing blue lights.
A fatal wreck. You can't turn away.
You sift through fragments,
carefully handling dangerous shards.
Piecing together what's left,
you make a new kind of mirror.

Therapy, Year Two

Only a few load-bearing timbers remain.
You hear the creak of nails
working loose.

Sleepless, Again

Tonight, I can't stop
touching the empty place
where the ring once was.

Fallen out of my orbit,
you have left me
wobbly.

Want swells up, and
the far reaches of regret
in moments that insist,
that won't be denied.

> *rain tapping against greenhouse glass*
> *your guitar sighing, put to bed in its case*
> *moonlit walk down cobblestone streets*
> *the undoing of a button*

I free-fall into old habits,
fretting mistakes like worry beads:
times I didn't measure up;
things I should have said, but didn't.

What do the stars say about shame?
What is the cloud's opinion on longing?

Held in the dark
by a language of loss,
I try counting what I am thankful for

incantation, a bridge
that helps me
cross from night to dawn.

From Green Ground

Way will open,
Quakers say,
but path is defined
by ways that close, too.

Standing outside
this locked door,
questions and answers
no longer matter.

Wrong words said,
right ones not—
no difference now.
These keys don't fit.

After so long,
separating
feels like falling,
or dying.

Starting over
from green ground,
you lean toward spareness.

Pay attention
to inclination.

Moving On

Make a path through furnishings.
Haul out trash and rubble.
Tattered issues of *Cooking Light*.
Scuffed pairs of worn-out boots.
Rusty hubcap, leaky raft.
Single earring, solo socks.

Sift through clutter, odds and ends,
things held on to past their time.
Three-legged chair you couldn't fix,
blow-dryer that never worked.
Yellowed spatulas, wooden spoons.
Empty old rooms. Let them be spacious.

From the garden, decide
what can and won't be divided.
You can transplant squash blossoms
and roses to your next place
where they may open white hearts
and a new world might bloom.

In the Space Provided Below, Tell Us About Yourself

After learning to dress myself, tie my shoes, and read,
I earned merit badges, diagrammed sentences,
sang second soprano in the choir.
Built hundreds of campfires by Coeur d'Alene Lake
where I took full deep breaths.
Attended three universities, accumulated student loans,
kissed 19 different guys one summer in Guadalajara.
Listened to Aretha belt out "R-E-S-P-E-C-T."
Fell in love, fell out of love, fell in love again.
Cooked spicy pork stew, added extra garlic and jalapeños.
Lied to myself, then tried not to any more.
Wore five different uniforms; outgrew all but one.
Held my mother's hand as she died. Didn't have children.
Heard a sail luffing, flapping its empty dream.
Hurt someone badly along the way.
Watched old women sit on porches in Bruges, tatting lace.
Found a good teacher. Quit biting my fingernails.
Lost pounds, gained some back.
Rotated my tires, but not very often.
Re-read *A Tree Grows in Brooklyn*,
wept for the things I didn't know.
Dreamed fence posts and barbed wire
far into the horizon. Danced
to the end of the page, then
over the margins into other stories.

II

We have come this far
this is given to us, to touch
each other in this way.

—Rainer Maria Rilke

Above the Garage Door, Facing East

a red clay sun's
cheerful eyes, open grin.
One windy March day
I catch her chewing
with her mouth open,
straws and twigs poking out.

In April she dreams
small heartbeats.
I hear peeps
through the wall,
nested in her smile.

Today, startled
when the garage door opens,
she blurts sparrows
into the slap of sky,
sudden birds
she would like to take back.

Sunflower Hill, Yakima

The sun wakes from another time,
rising along the earth's curve.
Morning begins again and so do we,
here in the house on the hill
that claimed us at first sight.

This place looked like hope to us.
Up a winding gravel road
where old roses bloom,
tanned hides of rolling hills,
Mt. Adams watching over all.

Only certain plants survive
this sun, tenaciously holding on.
Balsamroot, sage, and silence grow.
Grey-diggers scratch dry earth,
squirreling into holes.

Raspberries ripen before us.
Branches hang low,
heavy with peaches.
A few have fallen in the night,
bruised eggs in nests of orchard grass.

This is where we have come
with our years of age
and what we know,
with the questions we hold
with our shadows and dreams.

Cooking for You

Minced garlic hisses and crackles in olive oil.
Skillet about to smoke, I add diced tomatoes
and mushrooms, oregano and red pepper flakes.
Billie Holliday cooks her way through
"Ain't Nobody's Business if I Do,"
sax crooning. I toss chopped clams
into the mix, salt and pepper, let it simmer.
Whole-wheat linguini boils.
I am cooking for you again
dear, drizzling oil and vinegar and a squeeze of lemon
over salad greens, blueberries, apples.
Blue cheese and toasted pecans.
Uncorking the chardonnay, I pour us each a glass,
remembering you on that flat rock in
the McKenzie River one early summer day,
hot sun on bare skin, blue eyes dancing—
don't I know your beauty.
Then. Now. I double-pinch
fresh parsley into the love and plenty sauce,
drain and toss the pasta into the steaming skillet.

Here, Where Even the Rocks Have Names

Having traveled decades together,
the two are putting down roots.
Sagebrush and thistle mark craggy hills,
ground squirrels scrabble the dust.

Rising off the open field,
a circling hawk rides its thermal.
Conserves its energy for other things.

Earlier this year, their neighbor
cut away acres of trees.
Gala apples no longer exist.
Planted in their place,
flimsy vines of wine grapes
in long straight rows.
In time, Syrah will be bottled,
will improve with age.

Listening to trills from distant birds
they cannot name, the two try to imagine
ways they will take this place into them,
how it may shape what they become.

Waking From a Fruitful Sleep

full of seeds bursting with questions,
you turn and ask *Can I tell you my dream?*
Leaning into the lull of your voice,
I enter your wilderness.
Filled with shadows
and splashes of light,
you tell what you remember,
shimmering moments
only glimpsed in passing.
Ghosts you met and invited for tea,
some hungry and lonely.
There is only this moment:
your dream, a small fire, tended,
warming us with its flames.
Yes, you can tell me.
You can always tell me.

Windiest Spring We Can Recall

breezes into summer, too.
Leaves rustle and shiver,

limbs bend and sway
through dark tangles of trees.
Dry grasses rattle like a snake's warning.

Weeds tumble up against fence posts.
Broken branches litter the ground.
Songbirds go quiet and disappear.

Quail and pheasant scurry for cover
from relentless racket and din.

Two cedar shakes fly from our roof.
The rusty garbage can rolls

into a neighbor's cherry orchard.
In the desert, wind, like love,

is often too much or not enough.
It's hard for us to love

this wind,

to praise and bless it for what it is.
Tired of the howling loneliness
folks become edgy

(Enough already!)
wish for the wild scribble to dwindle,

settle to a murmur, a hush.
Impatient for its dying down,

for later, when sparrows will rest
and sing their consolation

into the silence.

The Dog & I Listen

I chop garlic, dice onions.
Ears lift when wheels crunch gravel.
Your arrival, still my favorite sound.

In Our Garden, the Smiling Stone Buddha

Sunlight breaks through
months of grey.
Blades pierce the soil,
spears of iris poke up
from bark chips,
daffodils trumpet yellow.

In our garden,
the smiling stone Buddha
reaches out open arms,
welcomes this carnival
of color and fragrance.

Simply open and receive he says,
pointing to days warming,
leaves greening,
new fruit forming,
and all this light.

Herbs

Scratching furrows with a stick
into hardpan soil, pinching in starts—
rosemary, parsley, cilantro, dill—
patting dirt into place with bare palms,
watering gently, like soft rain.
You believe in the spice that awaits us,
know this oregano, this thyme,
will flavor our lives.

Waking to Rain I Move Toward You

Sometimes you're already there when I turn
listening with softer ears
and what registers in you is *home*.

Other times your eyes, cool and distant,
remind that you, too,
have far and private places where no one else can go.

The quick and sudden sting
of your recent surgeries reminds us
we won't be here forever.
One of us will leave the other.
Let it be me, I pray, when fear prevails
against the now.

This anticipation does not serve me well.
What we're living is our life.
So I get on with it, remembering things, like litanies:

Whitewater rafting that almost ended badly.
A long conversation by a Christmas tree
that we thought would end differently.
A trio in the plaza near Antwerp Cathedral,
classical music wafting our outdoor café.
Nantucket scallops sizzling in butter,
sweet pink flesh, tender in garlic.

Holding separate strands together,
fingering them like knots on a string,
as if such memories could keep us safe,
as if they could save us.

Morning breathes its gray chill.
I move toward you.

Terrier

Holding the day loosely,
he asks nothing more of me
than I'm able to give.
Walk? Play? Suppertime?
Attention shifts to bird, to squirrel—
the next live thing inviting chase.
Unleashed from memory and prediction,
he pees on bushes and fence posts,
more theory than streams
marking his spots.
Nose fetches world
into realms of knowing.
Ears swivel to each small sound.
All we have is here, is now.
Tensing a haunch,
his raised tail, rippling muscle.

Plenty

Feathered in sunlight,
robins chatter on limbs,
telling lies about
biggest worms caught,
and which nests held
through last week's winds.

They brag about
this time last year
when they stripped
these trees clean
before we got around
to picking.

They are all in love
with July's
blushing Rainiers,
deep red Bings,

gorging themselves fat
on the sweet blood
of cracked hearts,
eating their fill.

Behind Lids of Half-Closed Eyes

My dead keep showing up
wearing clip-on earrings,
doing crosswords in ink,
offering striped peppermints
from a cut-glass dish.

They smell of Jergens and Polident,
read *Popular Mechanics* and *TV Guide,*
laugh at the jokes on *Hee Haw*
'til tears pour down their cheeks.

One of them is building
a crystal radio in the basement.
Another whistles "It's Such a Pretty World Today."
That one has become the watercolorist
she always wanted to be.

Each greets a faithful but fainter
version of my former self,
time thinning between dream and day.

Praise Song

Prayers and prayer life weigh heavily on me
as the only appropriate response to this life.
These countless taken for granted breaths every day.
—Jim Bodeen

Praise petals, praise stamen, praise pistil, praise pollen.
Bless your garden, a language of color
blooming delight and endless change.

Praise flashy finches darting the sky.
All that gold.

Praise the strength that comes from here. From now.
From sunrise, from jazz, from daily lines.
From the tea. The garden.
From this feeling.

Bless your weathering face.
No matter how dim or distant,
the possibilities all there,
swimming in your eyes.

Over three decades, the wonder
of you and poetry and the press
has brought us here, to this.

Already the raspberries ripen,
reminding that riches arrive
even with summer's passing.

While You're in D.C.

I think about the three-hour time difference.
I think about your meeting with the senator.
I think about Kramer's Bookstore and Coffee Shop,
in DuPont Circle, their motto that we love:
If we had a shower, you could live here.

I think about what I forgot to tell you
on the phone yesterday—Helen's confused
and confusing call from Assisted Living,
the "yes" letter I got from *Calyx,*
two pheasants preening in the cherry orchard,
the first iris blooming.
Our dog—ears flat, tail tucked—
moping and sighing while you're away.

I think about where you are, the poetry of that city,
imagine us there together, walking
arm in arm down a cobblestone street,
like a river under the stars.

Home, surrounded by things that remind me of you
(a basket, a sweatshirt, a candle, a bowl)
I think about how different you and I are.
Like square differs from round, round from square.
How it's been thirty years
of unbroken conversation across a scarred table.
How you see the me I can't bear to.

I want to know, a country apart,
same sun shining above both our heads,
what bracelets circle your wrist today
what your hand is reaching for
whether you hear church bells ringing.

Yakima Postcard, to Carel

Now it's July, abundantly.
All over the valley, cherry trees are letting go.
Branches hang low, weighted with ripeness.
Boughs bending, bending—
a kind of forgiveness curving toward us.

We're thinking of you in Olympia,
caring round-the-clock for Lynn
through this last, hardest part.
Doing all it takes
so the one you love most
can be home, with you,
where she belongs.
Giving your all,
the way a fruit tree empties itself,
then fills again, and again.

Here, mourning doves coo.
We stumble along rutted lanes of grass,
gleaning Bings, Rainiers, pie cherries, too.
Gathering what we can hold.

Giving Notice

For decades, they have noticed you giving.
Today you are giving them notice.

Standing here, trembling,
it is time to go, again.

Traveling the years with colleagues,
the work you did here mattered.
Ways you shaped the job.
Ways the job shaped you.

Your shoulders know the weight of things carried.

Swept along by the swiftly moving waters
of your own life,
you have begun to listen
to the stream
beneath the stream.

Time now, for change.

In the slowing, the gloaming—
a deepening.
Stillness and quiet enough
to receive
your next calling.

On This, the Shortest Day of the Year

In the heart
of my house,
the phone rings.
She talks for
a long time.
She doesn't say
what she means.
We hang up,
but the call
is not over.
In the long
cold winter ahead
she and I
won't be sharing
the weather of
this grief.

Evening on Schuller Grade

Orange light quiets the sky.
Color stains trees
into lengthening shade.

Lean back in your chair,
feet bare in tickling grass,
while the sun sinks behind the hill.

Sparrows flit
from limb to limb
in the orchard.

The smell of apples
becoming themselves
can ripen you, too.

Feel the air begin
to cool your shoulders,
kissing your face, blessing it.

Catch the earth's pulse
through the soles of your feet.
Listen to the dark arrive.

Fill your empty place
with this horizon.
Hold it all lightly,

like that. Just like that.
Sit here, home,
the taste of evening in your mouth.

A Consolation of Quails

60 meetings in 60 days
she calls to say.

Talk swerves.
She never really drank much.
Nothing in common
with the others.

She points to other relatives
who drank. A grandpa.
Three uncles.

Watching a family of quail
outside my window,
I try to remember
the name for a group of them.

Whatever I say is wrong.

After we hang up
I continue
our conversation
in my head.
I know she does, too.
We're like that.

August Ripening, Yakima Valley

Apricots fall from the tree.
Loosening, letting go,
they thud in soft orchard grass.

I used to know
what I was meant to do
but I am someone else now.

Momma and poppa quail scurry by
gathering nineteen scattered chicks,
while you herd data

into a grant, shaping a dream
to help poor children in our town.
I am here in this valley,

time passing by and Mt. Adams
and sagebrush and my breath
and the open sky.

Yakima's river of wind
stirs my restlessness.
In the present, in the present

I remind myself, waiting for the nudge,
giving wildness its chance,
but then, the slightest stiffening,

obstinacy, heels dug in
standing my ground.
Unclear about what's next,

unsure what it will take
to loosen, and let go, I wait.
Apricots fall from the tree.

Throat Praise in the Desert

We left the sprinkler on all night.
This morning, sparrows chatter and sing
bathing in the new small lake
they've found in basalt rock.
Their melodies say "This pool is ours."
Their state flower is beauty.
When they shake with joy,
my heart flutters, too,
celebrating the cool pleasure
of water held in stone.

This Is Where I Get to Thank You for Showing Me

How to move toward my tears.
Because breaking down
can mean breaking through.

How the poet's practice
matters more than the poem.

How to look up from my texts
and learn to read
the world.

And the open notebook
becomes a rudder.

What I'm talking about is
how to quiet my cleverness,
then listen.

What I'm talking about is
how to hear the call,
and respond.

And if there are those who snicker,
doubt, hint at self-serving—
they know nothing.

I'm talking about duende.
Desolation and desire.
Dark, floating, edgeless, deep.

Towards the bottom
are things
you have to believe
to see.

September Ripens and So Do We

Me, in the kitchen,
buttering slices of whole grain toast,
cracking fresh farm eggs
into a sizzling pan, admiring
deep-orange suns.

You, in the orchard,
bruised peach cradled in your hand
cupping its heaviness.
Standing there, caring,
holding all that sweetness.

Here on the Edge of Desert

I'd like to send you a morning like this.
Golden sun on stubbled fields,
hills tawny as a lion's flank.
Sage and stillness, sky and quiet.

I'd like to give you this
glimpse of clear blue
where two hawks circle,
riding thermals.

Offer you fists of flowers,
blooming in our garden:
hollyhocks, star lilies,
poppies and roses

scents carried on air
calling you home,
to things you left
but failed to get away from.

I'd like to invite you
to pluck ripe fruit
from our backyard tree,
feast on peach after peach.

When you hear these finches sing
songs that have to be sung,
feel them filling your lungs,
you'll know the gold is here.

"Peace is Everything in its Right Power"

14 year-old boy's response to the question
"What is peace?" in an NPR interview

The thrill of the dog pacing the backseat,
nose out the window, ears blown back,
panting-whimpering-wagging
when we cross the bridge
approaching the cabin.

The pleasure of keys on a ring,
toothed edges jangling in a pocket;
the way they fit the hollow of hand
holding the mystery of opening
made for that very purpose.

The satisfaction of white paper
in front of me, pen scratching
ink across the page
as I gradually let go of
the rest of the world.

The joy of sitting next to you
here in our living room
with books and tables and lamps
and paintings and orange star lilies
on an ordinary day of love.

III

World, World, I cannot get thee close enough!

—Edna St. Vincent Millay

Howling Like a Coyote

Are you authorized to speak
For these apple trees
Felled by roaring chainsaws
Acre after acre?
Are you able to explain
What the orchard means to do
With hundreds of stumps
Left in graveyard rows?
What it intends to make
Of this emptiness?
What do you know
About the fierce whirring
Of windmill blades on blue days,
Pickups parked along the irrigation ditch,
Smudge pots rusting away in weeds?
Who gave you permission
To look at beer cans and
Tumbleweeds rolling through?
At the *For Sale* sign in the widow's yard,
Faded laundry flapping on her line?
Ask yourself if poems are enough,
Or if you'd be better off
Slinking into the sagebrush
And howling like a coyote?

What Would it Take?

...like a fist clenched in anger but there is no impact.
No release. I'm not sure what it would take.
                                    —Anh-Hoa Thi Nguyen

The lava is in all of us.
Now, the floating her,

the missing her, rumbles.
That little girl, a prisoner

who surrendered because
she had no line of defense,

her body split, swallowed,
hollowed out, survived

by becoming a face others need.
Open arms, eyes, wallet, bed.

This ancient volcano runs deep.
She holds a pen.

Awake at 2:00 A.M.

Bobbing again on dark water,
pen in hand, I float

between night and dawn.
There is no moon.

Unmoored, rudderless,
I drift in silence, waiting.

Behind the sleeping door
my lover hugs her distant dream.

A small animal scurries inside
the length of our living room wall.

I scribble and scratch lines.
Words have saved lives,

helped prepare us for that time
when nothing will save us.

Tonight there is no moon.
White paper in front of me,

I send up my flimsy prayer,
ink rising off the page.

Shrine of the Pines

The postcard to Doug & Wendy in Maryland
sent from Dad, Bess & Company, shows
Bud Overholser's historic Missouri landmark
of over 200 artifacts hand-carved
from virgin pine stumps and roots.

> *Hi—we were here*
> *on Thurs. Picnicked*
> *at Pettibone Lake—*
> *visited the Pines*
> *& had ice cream*
> *in Baldwin*

The photo is a shack crawling with gnarled
bench legs and bony chair arms, stump end tables,
other wood furniture too, golden and curled, a nightmare
of roots twisting and winding like tentacles, like snakes,
tangled into questions, knotted like problems.
Deer heads stare from every wall, their antlers
echoed in each carved object in the room.

Bud built this as a shrine, but to what?
And which meaning of the word did he have in mind?
A sacred or holy place, like temple or tabernacle?
A reliquary or repository? Or, more chilling—
tomb, burial chamber, mausoleum?
Busy and claustrophobic, at first this darkened den
strikes me as the latter, a bandit's hideaway,
or the hermit shelter of The Unabomber.

What kind of person imagined such a place?
And why, Bud? *Why?* Did you love
those virgin pines so much you cut them down?
Or, stumbling upon these roots and stumps, feel called
to create something from them,
in homage, or as prayer?

Looking longer, I begin to glimpse
the shrine's strange beauty,
begin to give Bud the credit he deserves
for taking what was given,
and making what he could from it.

Sipping Coffee in His Backyard Garden

under dipping branches, canopies of leaves
greener than before, she writes lines,
pages, brimming.

Each morning offers new surprises—
what lifts and rises from mud and muck.
Today, the first English Breakfast radishes.
Foxgloves' purple buzzing with bees,
mums announcing their yellow.
The holy hunger of hummingbird
dipping into calyx.

A black and white cat yawns and
stretches in its stripe of sunlight.

The woman has been looking
for places she feels at home.
Here she thinks, his tended blossoms.
And new paths he is making
from gravel and stone.

Starting

Sometimes it begins
with a stirring that urges
and leads you on, like
a stream feeling its way
toward the ocean
into which it will empty.

Sometimes it's coaxing
notes from a guitar,
the plucked string,
reverberating.

It's untangling knots of dreams,
combing shores for shells,
plucking fruit from limbs.

Sometimes the light is in you
as you name yourself.

And when it works, there's the gift
of someone else nodding,
I've felt that, too.

November Morning, Useless Bay, Halfway Through a Month-Long Writing Residency on Whidbey Island

Sparrows punctuate the wire,
singing early songs.
Shoes slap pavement
still wet from last night's storm,
step over slugs slicking new trails,
past a dead field mouse
that just looks asleep,
wren lost to a windshield,
feathers tattered.
By the road, plump blackberries
glisten, ripe for picking.
Reaching into the tangle
for a handful of easy ones,
you taste the burst of sweet
black juice, swallow, smile.
Around the bend, velvet acres of cattails.
From the marsh dozens of geese rise
honking a frenzied chorus
aiming their V into the sky.
Not hesitating to start,
not worrying which way to go.

Invitation

Say pebble, say button, say spoon.
Say table, say scissors, say bowl.
Thimble. Pillow. Toast.
Kettle. Pepper. Lamp.
When one issues an invitation,
accept with a grateful *yes*.

Say stem and stalk.
Bark, sap, needles, leaves
from maple, hemlock, cedar.
Say sycamore.
Now say it again.
Sycamore.

Hear the question
each word asks
and then go on from there.
Birds folded away.
Staccato heels clicking.
Cold water sipped from a tin cup.

Find it, lose it,
find it again.
Be patient.
There is no rush.
Each will tell you
where it wants to go.

Reading/Writing Notebook

Like any good teacher,
it both leads and follows.

It softens hard edges,
springs hinges loose.

Unfastens bolts rusted tight.
Sheds light down long corridors.

Announces deafening omissions.
Unfurls rolled flags.

Provides fingerprints,
offers up evidence.

Soothing as sweetgrass,
it tips toward fullness.

Gathering, We Remember

> *Together we will love this beautiful,*
> *broken world of which we are a part.*
> —Terry Tempest Williams

Traveling a country for which
we've long been homesick,
something has been set in motion.
Unearthing things we'd blindly felt,
holding them up to the light,
we are writing for our lives.
Foundations tremble and groan.
Ancient plates shift deep below—
the moving earth beneath us
a rocking & rolling reminder
that we all walk on shaky ground.
I call up your voices reading your stories,
see you lean in, listening,
recalling something forgotten,
waiting for what you don't yet know.

The Third Wrestler Cries

Never the football players.
Never the basketball players.
No baseball or track or soccer guys.
Only the wrestlers.

Jaime is the third.
Freshman coiled tight as a spring,
biceps bulging under t-shirt,
here during my office hour wanting
to talk about the Sherman Alexie poem
he has chosen for his class presentation.

All earnestness, gaze direct, he practices
reading it aloud, knee bouncing
up and down like a jackhammer.
When he reaches a line that moves him,
lips tremble and he halts, unable to continue.
Brown eyes look up at me, liquid pools
teeming, startled fish about to spill over.
"See, I *get* this guy" he tells me, voice cracking.

Jaime, I'm not as hungry as you,
spitting and sweating and starving away
those last three pounds, trying
to make weight by Thursday.
Not as tired as you,
dark circles ringing your eyes.
But believe me: *I get you, too.*
See, I know about intensity—
its blessing and its curse.
Know the pressure of one-on-one,
how it feels to be alone out there,
on the mat, in the spotlight,
facing that next opponent.

And isn't the point to love—
even if too much, or the wrong way?
To lose yourself in what you do
in hopes of finding yourself?
Listening, nodding, I shove
the Kleenex box across the desk,
offer the tissue.

Giving the Test

Pens scratch across white, leaving tracks in snow.
Meghan hunches, forehead in hand, squints at the marks,
deciphering. Fabian sighs, shoots me a glare
that says "This is all your fault, you know."
Jeff looks up at the ceiling,
Julie stares out the window,
Cody taps his pen.

Watching them, I think of the narrator of this play,
who's a character in it, too. Insider and outsider,
like I am here, slipping and sliding in and out of the margins.

I love these damaged characters,
burning with the fires of human desperation,
mirroring each of us in their dignity and tragic beauty.
The controlling mother, making plans and provisions,
unable to face the facts. Stuck in the past,
she clings to what she can never have again.
A daughter, too fragile to move from the shelf,
limping along in painful self-consciousness.
The absent father, a telephone man
who fell in love with long distance.
The emissary from the outside world, one brief breath
of fresh air for this closed-off, musty family.
The trapped son, nailed into a premature coffin.
His desire for freedom in the midst of duty.
To save himself, he must act without pity,
but he will be haunted by this for the rest of his life.

It's the larger questions that interest me, ones too big
for this one small exam. But they're eighteen years old.
And we've got fifty minutes. So we do the best we can.

The real test, the one I can't give, but that
will be given, asks harder questions:
In what ways are you "crippled" or fragile?
What have you lost? What do you miss?
Where do you cling too tightly?
Is just a little happiness and good fortune
too much to ask for? Is it enough?
Have you felt, or do you feel, trapped in some way?
What must you do to save yourself?
Do you have regrets that haunt you?
("If not yet, you will," I want to tell them).

Laurie's eyes wander toward Michael's paper.
She catches my stare, squirms, regains her focus.
Miguel's left knee bounces up and down,
while Nicole searches for right words
at the bottom of her Starbucks cup.
They are remembering a world
where everything happened to music.

My affection for them washes over the room
like a slanted beam of light.
I wish you luck—and happiness—and success!
All three—

Office Hours

Fall Quarter

Julie, who will be student teaching next quarter, comes by to talk to me. The form from the Placement Office asks her to list her permanent address, and she's unsure what to do. Her parents are homeless, have been living on the street somewhere in Seattle, she doesn't know where. She worries about them, wonders if she'll ever be able to find them, and, if she does, what then? "But for now, what should I write on the form?" she asks.

Winter Quarter

Marie calls to tell me she probably won't be able to make it to methods class today. She sounds shaken. When I ask her if she's all right, she says, "No, I'm really not"—tells me that in the middle of the night a man smashed her second story window, broke into her apartment, and raped her. She has been sitting alone in her living room ever since, staring at the wall, shivering. She hasn't told anyone until now, when she realized she really should let me know that she might be missing class this afternoon.

Spring Quarter

Matt is waiting outside my office when I arrive. He reaches for the stack of books and briefcase I am carrying and holds them while I unlock the door. "How was your spring break?" I ask. "Not good," he says, closing it behind us. Face pale, he describes his week. He was diagnosed with AIDS on Monday, and on Wednesday, drove to his small rural hometown to break the news to his parents—not only that he is sick, but that he is gay. He describes his mother's pain, his father's rage, his own fear. When he finishes telling his story, I stand, hug him, hold him. Then close the door behind him, and gather myself for my next class.

Thirty Years Later, I Defend My Dissertation All Night in a Dream & Wake Up Exhausted

Midterm week on campus. Tightrope nerves, temperatures rising.
Tension, thick as fog. Students bump into things,
dazed and startled, red eyes open too wide,
night animals caught in unexpected headlights.

In the hallway, Sara June bursts into tears
when I offer her a piece of dark chocolate.
Don't be too nice to me right now, OK?

Ross comes by my office, sweat pebbling his pink forehead,
concerned about his tone in the midpoint course evaluation.
I hope I didn't sound harsh. I really _like_ this class.

Marie, a teary freshman, stops in to tell me
she has applied for a hardship withdrawal.
Money problems at home, her grandma just died
and well, I had an abortion last week.
My mom was really supportive, because
the same thing happened to her when she was eighteen.
But my dad doesn't know.

Predictable, but unsettling, this time of the quarter stirs shadows.
Wishing we could all apply for hardship withdrawals,
I listen, and breathe.

Working the Booth at Aunties' Fireworks

This is red, white and blue Americana,
land of the brave, home of the free
where happiness is the bang, the explosion,
is blowing things up, where sulfur smells
like testosterone and college boys ask
for bottle rockets, firecrackers, cherry bombs—
illegal stuff only sold on the rez, then disappointed,
want what's biggest, loudest, most extreme.
"Easy fellas. You know, women like it slower," we joke.
Where husbands pick out the big cakes—
Black Cat, Pyro Tech, Grand Finale—
put them on the table for purchase,
and their wives put them back on the shelf,
suggest kid stuff instead—snaps, snakes,
tanks, "sparklers and fountains are pretty."
But the men want missiles, repeating shells, multi-shot aerials,
want roman candles they can hold in their hand,
ejaculating sparks of light and loud reports.
The men want biggest, brightest, panoplies of color,
pleasing to the eye, but loud, too. We throw in
a box of matches and their promise,
give out punks for free. Working the booth,
we learn about men and beauty
and its draw—chrysanthemums and anemones,
credit card and beer-fueled artillery,
the fizzling, sparkling, fiery wheels,
leaving red casings, carcasses of split cakes
in their stunned aftermath.

What Does It Take to Change a Town?

Only sand. For six days, I've watched
five Tibetan monks of Drepung Loseling
lean easily over a raised square platform
hour after hour in open concentration,
tapping fine lines of colored sand.

Holding a chakpur in one hand, each runs
a metal rod along the funnel's grated surface.
Herbs flow like liquid, sound like a chant.
This art is prayer. Grain by grain,
the monks tap colors of intention.

Men who embrace peace carry themselves differently.
I could love them, I think, kind unlined faces,
eyes like grandmothers', compact bodies draped
in flowing maroon robes. Could run my hand
across soft black bristles of brush-cut hair,
bury my nose in brown necks, smooth as wind.
They summon tenderness.

What will those of us who have learned
to hold on tightly with both hands
take away? At the end of the week
they sweep the table clean
scattering colorful grains to the sea.

Clearing Out the Judge's Cabin

Look for answers you can't find in cluttered drawers—
plaid boxer shorts, striped pajamas, moth-eaten sweaters.
On shelves, law books he won't go back to, tattered mysteries,
an ancient dictionary, covered in dust.
Save *Peterson's Field Guide to Western Birds* and
the fly-tying manual, still useful, here on the river.
Toss old playing cards, greasy from wear,
but not two decks still wrapped in cellophane,
or patriotic boxes of poker chips.
Trash keys to locks lost or forgotten.
Pass photos and news clippings to those who knew him.
Dump river stones and petrified wood collected on long hikes.
Give away leather boots with worn soles.
Hand off the warped bookcase leaning in the corner,
the patched recliner that doesn't fit your body.
Set aside the garish painting of the wooded scene;
you may want it later.
The elk horns go, as do the lampshades.
Save Patsy Cline, Johnny Cash, and Willie Nelson,
but remove the rickety record player.
Hang on to the brass keychain, embossed with
the seal of a governor who served seven terms back.
Out with the empty champagne bottle on the
fireplace mantle, the plaque in the kitchen reading
The only difference between men and boys is the price of their toys.
From kitchen cupboards, throw out ancient spices,
rancid oils, cloudy tabasco.
Save users' manuals for the stove and fridge.
Hang on to mouse and yellow jacket traps.
Remove the steel chamber pot under the upstairs bed.
Get rid of rusty razor, shaving cream,
aspirin, long expired. The floss can go, too.
Keep the old tools hanging on the shed walls,
wooden handles worn smooth by his hands.
Move the old man out, leaving just enough
to say he was here.

A Question of Rivers

The care of rivers isn't a question of rivers,
but of the human heart.

—Tanaka Shozo

The pine tree lacks ambition.
The wild rose longs for nothing.

Restless as wind, thirst unsated, voice hollow,
I've come to let the river work on me.
Breeze whispers through evergreens.
Current rushes on like it always has.
Finches swoop and glide in pairs,
untouchable gold at their centers.

A chattering chipmunk scrabbles dust,
comes close to get a better look
at this strange newcomer,
her head in the clouds.
Stopping next to my foot,
he cocks his head,
clear eyes curious, wondering.

To do anything entirely,
with whole attention, is prayer.
Wild mind pinballs
from thought to thought,
past and future squeezing out now.
My restlessness is a script
I must learn to read.

What You Think About Rafting Through the Grand Canyon on the Eighth Day of Rain

Call it lightning, call it thunder, call it wind,
the canyon says *You need to know this.*

Teeth chattering, you remember
other canyons, smaller gulches, gorges, gullies.
You think of chasm, fissure, cleft and gap,
how notch and split can lead to opening.

Carrying little, pockets empty, you think about
the world behind and its comforts—
hot water, clean clothes, dry beds—
of mornings slept through, food eaten without tasting,
the sleepwalking trance of inattention
that domesticity allows.

Wet and shivering in your yellow raft,
you know this river's path
is the only one imaginable now.
There is no turning back.

Scuffed and bruised, you think about
flooding arroyos and washes,
torrents of mud and gravel, water roaring,
pouring down red cliffs into the roiling river.
About thunder louder and clouds darker
than you've heard or seen before,
about grey sky and brown water
you know could swallow you.

Approaching Crystal Rapid, you tighten your life jacket
and think of trusting guides and what they know,
how they read in water what you can't see.

On the eighth day of rain,
you think about how a storm, too, can be a poem.

And you look forward to day's end, when, cold and tired,
you and your friends will pull to a new shore,
unload gear, set up the kitchen, pitch tents, pour wine.
How you'll shake wet sand from your shoes,
how staccato raindrops will punctuate your tent,
how the next rapid's song will lull you to sleep.

End of March

Sun beginning
to break through.
Like an old dog
starting his day,
you stretch and groan,
opening
to what will come.
In this slow unfurling,
belief blossoms.
Another morning.
One more chance
to do what you can.

First of the Season

This morning, tulips explode,
like that spring your mother lay dying
when the first bright bursts
in her rock garden caused
your breath to catch and bloom—
vibrant hues igniting, rising
like flames, like fireworks;
yellow, orange, and red insisting
on beauty, on living, on yes, on more.

Worn Down by Internal Chatter, on a Country Road, Narrow and Winding

I walk until breath responds to landscape,
surrounded by the reassuring sameness of hills
curved one behind the other.

Sheep raise their heads at the sound
of my shoes slapping pavement
but they don't stop chewing.

Barn cat sprawls in a ribbon of sunlight,
his beautiful disinterest, taking whatever comes
without making a problem of it. Beyond all this caring.

Beside the ditch, sunflowers bow their heads.
A ruby throated hummingbird hesitates at a blossom.
Even the smallest thing has its sacred hungers.

Reading Basho in Our Valley

When I smell the sage release green heat
Hear pheasants flutter on the rise
See the sun shine orange on Mt. Adams
Even in Yakima
I long for Yakima.

Hiking Naches Heights

The absent ones follow me
on this trail,
stepping carefully
over roots and rocks,
not wanting to disturb.

Together we walk
past scraggle of underbrush,
past bramble, thistle, sage.
Past dipping limbs
in cherry orchards.
Tangled branches.
Brief blossoms.

Past the quail
perched on a fence post,
black plume quivering,
calling his warning
to the covey feeding below.

Last night, in the dark,
an incessant chorus
of crickets and frogs
carried me to another time,
a different place.
There, under a cuticle of moon,
I tasted regret, let it
linger on my tongue.

Memory is like that:
a lilac's fragrance,
a single acorn, a spoon,
still stirring—
and in that moment
you are who you once were,
not knowing
how much will disappear.

In Motion

Life is in motion—we are in motion—
even the stones are in motion.
—M.C. Richards

Finches chatter, magpies scold,
but the roses keep quiet about it.
These birds remember you weren't always here.
They keep trying to teach you things.

There is the moving silence of trees,
sustaining as breath.
Bones swept clean by wind.
How, in the breeze, sagebrush trembles.

Between images, between words,
a spacious, empty place.
Beyond all learning, habit, thought—
your original face, your true voice.

Like bones and sagebrush
and even the stones,
you will be carried forward.
You, yourself, are under way.

Notes on the Poems

This book's title and epigraph are from lines in William Stafford's poem, "The Dream of Now" in *Passwords*. HarperCollins Publishers, Inc. New York, NY, 1991.

The Gabriel García Márquez quote in the dedication is from Peter H. Stone's author interview in *Paris Review*, "The Art of Fiction No. 69."

The Adrienne Rich epigraph beginning section one is from her poem "Images for Godard," in *Collected Early Poems: 1950-1970*. W.W. Norton & Co., Inc. 1993.

SUNDAY DRIVE appeared in my first chapbook, *Wishboats*, published by Blue Begonia Press in 2000.

TWELVE is for Susan Wynstra, Eve Luppert, Jean Carter, and Mike Barber—Sacajawea Junior High alumni who are still my friends forty-*five* years later.

The book in THAT SUMMER I READ *DANDELION WINE* is by the late great Ray Bradbury, published by Doubleday in 1957. The song is "Black Water" by the Doobie Brothers, first released as the B-side of "Another Park, Another Sunday" and then on the album *What Were Once Vices Are Now Habits*.

WHEN MY SISTER CUT FRENCH CLASS is for Tam Martin, who not only made it to Paris but has traveled all seven continents.

HER HAIR IS RED is after Shari Stoddard's blind contour drawing with ink and water-soluble pastels exhibited in Sara Spurgeon Gallery, 2011.

THERAPY, YEAR TWO was written in response to visual artist Delma Tayer's collage/painting "Into the Chasm" as part of the Allied Arts collaborative Text & Image Exhibit in 2011.

SLEEPLESS AGAIN was written in response to jeweler Sally Von Bargen's "Clouds and Companions" brooch/necklace in sterling silver, wood, brass, digital prints on aluminum, and gold leaf as part of Facere Gallery's *Signs of Life: Contemporary Jewelry, Art, and Literature* collaborative text/image exhibit and publication in Seattle in 2010.

FROM GREEN GROUND and SIPPING COFFEE IN HIS BACKYARD GARDEN are for Mike Barber.

MOVING ON is for Sara Gettys.

The Rainer Maria Rilke epigraph beginning section two is from his second "Duino Elegy." *In Praise of Mortality: Selections from Rainer Maria Rilke's Duino Elegies and Sonnets to Orpheus*, translated and edited by Anita Barrows and Joanna Macy, Riverhead Books, 2005.

TERRIER memorializes Rudy, the old soul Buddha dog, not Vinny, the first-time-arounder.

YAKIMA POSTCARD, TO CAREL is for Carel Camerer, in loving memory of Lynn Damiano, 1961-2012.

PRAISE SONG and THIS IS WHERE I GET TO THANK YOU FOR SHOWING ME are for Jim Bodeen.

GIVING NOTICE is for Barb Mertens.

The Edna St. Vincent Millay epigraph beginning section three is from her poem "God's World" in *Renascence and Other Poems* published by Harper & Brothers, 1917. Thanks to prom date Steve Franks for the Sandy Dennis memoir which included it.

HOWLING LIKE A COYOTE borrows form from Charles Simic's "Carrying on Like a Crow."

WHAT WOULD IT TAKE? is for Anh-Hoa Thi Nguyen—poet, artist, Hedgebrook sister.

SHRINE OF THE PINES came about thanks to Wendy Call, whose postcard from her aunt and uncle issued the invitation.

GATHERING, WE REMEMBER is for students in the spring quarter English 366: Advanced Creative Nonfiction class the year we felt the earthquake.

WHAT YOU THINK ABOUT RAFTING THE GRAND CANYON ON THE EIGHTH DAY OF RAIN is for Jennifer Solmssen and Glenise McKenzie, with thanks for the adventure of a lifetime.

In A QUESTION OF RIVERS the idea "To do anything entirely, with whole attention, is prayer" borrows from Simone Weil ("Absolutely unmixed attention is prayer") in "Attention and Will." *Gravity and Grace*, trans. by Emma Craufund. First English edition published by Routledge, and Kegan Paul, London, 1952.

Acknowledgments

I am grateful to the editors of the following publications in which these poems (some in earlier versions) first appeared:

Rattle: When My Sister Cut French Class
Calyx: Behind Lids of Half-Closed Eyes
Cirque: A Question of Rivers; Sipping Coffee in His Backyard
    Garden
Seems: Pants on Fire
Glassworks Magazine: What Does it Take to Change a Town?
Grey Sparrow Journal: In Our Garden, the Smiling Stone Buddha
Oregon East: Entering the Question This Night Asks
Earth's Daughters: What If, Picking Out Her Headstone; Office
    Hours; That Summer I Read *Dandelion Wine*; Working the
    Booth at Aunties' Fireworks
Catamaran Literary Reader: Backyard
Rockhurst Review: Waking from a Fruitful Sleep
Sinister Wisdom: While You're in D.C.; Here, Where Even the Rocks
    Have Names; Yakima Postcard, to Carel
Paper Nautilus: Hiking Naches Heights
Parting Gifts: Dreams; August Ripening, Yakima Valley
RiverRun: Terrier
Whirlwind Review: Starting
Off the Coast: Worn Down by Internal Chatter, on a Country Road,
    Narrow and Winding
Windfall: Clearing Out the Judge's Cabin; Sunflower Hill
Spindrift: End of March; In Motion; Here on the Edge of Desert;
    Peace is Every Thing in its Right Power; November Morning,
    Useless Bay
Floating Bridge Review: Cooking for You; Root Canal; Reading/
    Writing Notebook
Cascade: The Power of Movies to Disturb
Stringtown: Waking to Rain I Move Toward You; Plenty; September
    Ripens, and So Do We
Crosscurrents: Her Hair Is Red; What Would it Take?
Poetry Pacific: Sorrow
Bijou Poetry Review: Bedtime; Reading Basho in Our Valley

Four and Twenty: Broom; The Dog and I Listen
Signs of Life: Contemporary Jewelry, Art, and Literature: Sleepless,
    Again
The Far Field: Evening on Schuller Grade
Poets of the American West Anthology: Moving On; September Ripens,
    and So Do We
Impact: An Anthology of Short Memoirs: In the Space Provided
    Below, Tell Us About Yourself
This Assignment is So Gay Anthology: The Third Wrestler Cries;
    Giving the Test
A Sense of Place Geospatial Anthology: Howling Like a Coyote
Ultra Short Memoirs Anthology: On This, the Shortest Day of the
    Year; A Consolation of Quails
Music in the Air Anthology: Here on the Edge of Desert
Keys to Silence Anthology: Sunday Drive
Daring to Repair Anthology: What Does it Take to Change a Town?;
    Therapy, Year Two; What Would it Take?
A Distance Too Great: Poems from the Grand Canyon Anthology: What
    You Think About Rafting Through the Grand Canyon on the
    Eighth Day of Rain

"Entering the Question This Night Asks," "Behind Lids of Half-
Closed Eyes," "A Question of Rivers," "Peace is Every Thing in its
Right Power," and "Cooking for You" won 1st place in the Allied
Arts Regional Poetry Contest in 2009. Thanks to Allied Arts for
years of supporting our fine community of poets in the Yakima
Valley.

Special thanks to Dan and Amy Peters of Blue Begonia Press for
their enthusiasm, generosity, and support for this project, and for
friendship in poetry. Honoring the history and spirit of the press,
founded by Jim and Karen Bodeen, Dan and Amy have made Blue
Begonia their own. I'm honored to be in their good company.

Thanks to Hedgebrook for a nurturing and productive residency
early on that made a real difference, and to Central Washington
University for their generous support during the writing of this book.

I am grateful to the following poets who provided me with ideas, insights, invitations, feedback and direction: Lucinda Roy, Lorna Dee Cervantes, Yusef Komunyaaka, Erin Belieu, Kim Stafford, Illya Kaminsky and Nikky Finney.

This book has benefited in untold ways from the close reading, good advice, and ready help of friends and fellow writers Elizabeth Austen, Jim Bodeen, Dan Peters, and Leonard Orr. Thanks to Rob Prout for joyful collaboration and for his dedication to the process of making this book's cover a thing of beauty; to Bob Fisher for capturing the light and helping the rest of us see it, too; and to Gary Miller for taking and sharing the candid author photo.

Thanks to my father, Lanney, and my sister, Tam, for deep roots and steadfast love.

A writer in stiff need of bucking up could find no better allies than my friends, advocates, and chosen family—Jean Carter and Mike Barber.

Thanks to friend and colleague Patsy Callaghan for a quarter century of carpool conversation—about Lynda Barry, politics, garage bands, *The Believer*, sisters, veterinary clinics, Adrienne Rich, the Catholic Church, saying yes & saying no, Jazz Alley, PTSD, wildness/wilderness, nursing homes, C.J. Cregg, the inherited piano, racism, sensible shoes, teaching, being daughters, David Foster Wallace, hot flashes, screen time, gay weddings, *Parenthood*, macaroni & cheese, and much more.

Finally, the word *hearth* holds the word *heart*. Many of the poems in section two are for Jane Gutting, who is home to me.

About the Author

Terry Martin earned a B.A. from Western Washington University and M.A. and Ph.D. from the University of Oregon. She's been fortunate to make her living reading, writing, and talking with students for 35+ years. An English Professor at Central Washington University, she is the recipient of CWU's Distinguished Professor Teaching Award and the CASE/Carnegie U.S. Professor of the Year Award. Her poems, essays, and articles have appeared in hundreds of publications and she has edited books, journals and anthologies. Her first book of poems, *Wishboats*, won the Judges' Choice Award at Seattle's Bumbershoot Book Fair in 2000. Her second book, *The Secret Language of Women*, was published by Blue Begonia Press in 2006. She lives with her family in Yakima, Washington.